LIKE ME LIKE YOU

Zack Has
ASTHMA

JILLIAN POWELL

CHELSEA CLUBHOUSE
An Imprint of Chelsea House Publishers
A Haights Cross Communications Company
Philadelphia

Hi, my name is Zack and I have **asthma**. It means I sometimes find it hard to breathe. The doctors found out I had asthma when I was very young.

ASTHMA

Asthma makes the **airways** to the lungs narrower so it is harder to breathe.

I live with my mom, brother, and sister. They all have asthma, too. We keep some fish as pets. I would like to have a dog, but we can't, because animal **dander** can make our asthma worse.

7

We live near the ocean. We often go for walks along the beach, and I sometimes play soccer there, too. I like being out in the fresh air.

ASTHMA TRIGGERS

- Infections like colds
- Dirty air or smoke
- House-dust mites
- Plant pollen
- Animal dander (flakes of skin and saliva)
- Changes in the weather

We have to be careful to keep our house clean, because the **mites** that live in **house-dust** are very bad for our asthma. We all take turns at cleaning and vacuuming!

9

I have special covers on my bed to keep house-dust mites away. Mom vacuums the bed once a week, too.

She also washes all my sheets and pillowcases in very hot water to kill any house-dust mites.

HOUSE-DUST MITES

House-dust mites are very small and can only be seen through a **microscope**. This picture shows a house-dust mite enlarged to more than a thousand times its real size!

11

I take medicine every day for my asthma. Before I take my medicine in the morning, I blow into a **peak flow meter**. It measures how open the airways to my lungs are. I take a deep breath in, then blow out hard into the meter. I blow into the meter three times.

Then I write down my highest level on a chart. I show the chart to the nurse when I go for a checkup at the asthma clinic. I have a checkup four times a year. The nurse listens to my breathing, weighs and measures me, and checks that I'm using my inhaler the right way.

I take my asthma medicine twice a day. I breathe it in through my **preventer inhaler**. I put the inhaler into my mouth, then press it and take a puff of medicine. When I was younger, I used a **spacer device** to take my medicine. I still use one sometimes when my asthma is bad.

After I use my inhaler, I brush my teeth and wash out my mouth in case there is any medicine left in it. I have to remember to take my medicine again at night before I go to bed.

Today I'm going to play soccer for my team. I pack my **reliever inhaler** in my sports bag. I use this inhaler when my asthma is bad. It contains medicine that helps me breathe more easily. I take my reliever inhaler everywhere I go and keep a spare one in my desk at school.

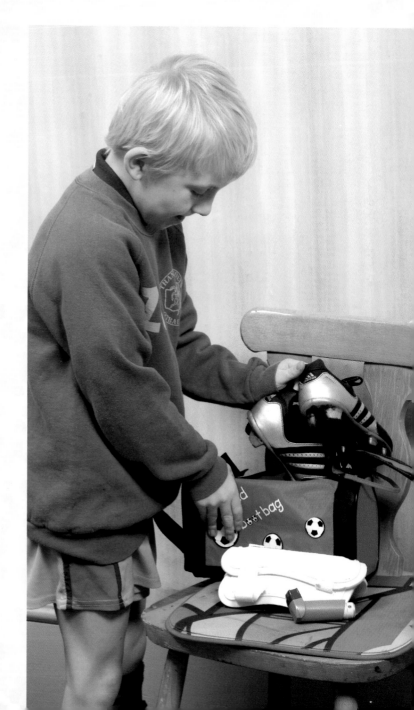

I love soccer and play it whenever I can. My own soccer team won a trophy this year, because we came in second out of twenty-four teams!

Today we're playing against a team from a nearby town. I'm playing defense. It's hard work but I really enjoy it!

After a while, I start to feel a bit wheezy. The coach replaces me so I can have a rest. The grass has been cut and that makes my asthma worse. My chest feels tight and I'm coughing.

ALLERGIES

Many children who have asthma also have **allergies** such as **hay fever** or food allergies.

I have to use my reliever inhaler. It's a different color from the preventer inhaler, so I don't get them mixed up. I'm using a spacer device with the inhaler to help get the medicine to my lungs more quickly.

20

It takes about ten minutes for the reliever medicine to work. My teammates, Robert and Matthew, come over at halftime to ask how I'm feeling.

21

Mom asks me if I'm feeling a little better now. She can also tell if I'm getting better by feeling my back to see if my breathing is getting easier.

ONE IN EIGHT

About one in eight children have asthma.

After a while, the wheezing stops and I feel ready to join in the game again. I wait with the coach until it's time to go back on to the field.

I'm always really hungry after playing soccer! At home, Mom makes us a snack while I tell my sister Carleigh all about the game.

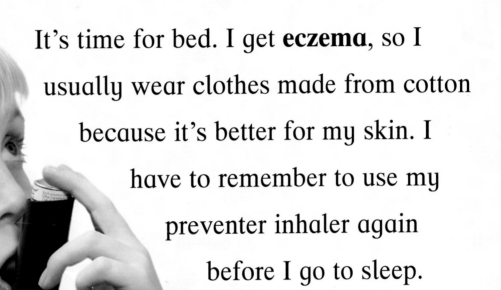

It's time for bed. I get **eczema**, so I usually wear clothes made from cotton because it's better for my skin. I have to remember to use my preventer inhaler again before I go to sleep.

ECZEMA

Eczema is common in children who have asthma. It's a skin condition that causes itching and rashes.

25

The worst thing about having asthma is when it's bad and I have to rest. But most of the time, I can do what I like. I love running, playing soccer, and doing other sports.

The best thing is going on special trips for children with asthma! We always have lots of fun and it's great making friends with other children who have asthma, too.

> Some children grow out of asthma when they reach their teens.

27

Glossary

Airways the tubes that carry air into and out of the lungs

Allergies when the body reacts badly to a trigger such as food, pollen, or dust

Asthma a condition that can cause problems with breathing, such as coughing and wheezing

Dander flakes of skin and saliva

Eczema a condition that causes a rash and itching; it can be an allergy

Hay fever allergy caused by plant pollen

House-dust mites small creatures that live in household dust

Inhaler something that is used to breathe medicine into the lungs

Microscope an instrument that makes things look bigger then they are

Peak flow meter a meter that measures how open the airways to the lungs are

Preventer asthma medicine taken every day to try and prevent asthma

Reliever medicine that helps make breathing easier when asthma has started

Spacer device a plastic container that fits over the mouth and makes it easier to use an inhaler

Index

Further Information

American Lung Association (ALA)
800-586-4872
www.lungusa.org/asthma
Lots of facts and information on asthma,
including asthma in children.

Allergy & Asthma Network Mothers of Asthmatics
800-878-4403
www.aanma.org
National nonprofit network of families whose
desire is to overcome allergies and asthma in
their children.

Allergy, Asthma & Immunology Online
http://allergy.mcg.edu
An information and news service maintained
by allergists, this site provides clinical health
information for adults and children.

National Asthma Education and Prevention Program
301-592-8573
www.nhlbi.nih.gov/about/naepp
Works to educate parents, health professionals,
and the public about asthma.

BOOKS
Sportsercise: A School Story about Exercise-Induced Asthma, Kim Gosselin et al.,
JayJo Books, 2004

What Your Doctor May Not Tell You about Children's Allergies and Asthma: Simple Steps to Help Stop Attacks and Improve Your Child's Health, Paul Ehrlich et al.,
Warner Books, Incorporated, 2003

The Complete Kid's Allergy and Asthma Guide: Allergy and Asthma Information for Children of All Ages, Milton Gold,
Robert Rose Incorporated, 2003

Asthma, Sharon Gordon,
Scholastic Library Publishing, 2003